Pieces inspired by and about Hip Hop

Naila Mattison-Jones
©2001
Impact Publishing.Net 2002
Philadelphia PA

Cover Design & Illustrations James Jones ©2001
Cover Photo by Tito Irizarry
"naila who?" Photo by Jayson Musson

This Book is Dedicated
To

Emmanuel - because your love of music reminds me of its importance
Nana - I miss you

Thanx

mom - i love and respect you so much more than i could ever tell you, my two dads; kevin - thank you for throwing my nwa tape out the window driving down route 10, the dialogue that began that day is absolutely the foundation of this collection. miles - for being you and reminding me to find paths where it seems that none exist. true - i love you and your undying support is what gets me out of bed most mornings. emmanuel - my whole world is yours. to the rest of my family, pop-pop, uncle gregory & aunt faith, jay, heather - who allowed me to take you to a roots show then acted like you didn't want to come home!!!, grandmom, khalil, dominique, carole. thank you for putting up with me. the poole family - for welcoming me with open arms.

rich medina and stephanie renée, my adoptive big brother and sister - thank you both for listening and also puttin' a foot in my ass when i needed one. jayson - you now have a companion for swords if you ever choose to re-release your satirical masterpiece. nandi - for everything. stacey wilson and stef tetas - for being there as reminders that all people must be taken on an individual basis, i just really dig both of y'all. to the crew formerly known as the foreign objects, thank you for exposing me to a whole other side of the game. adam and tito - for taking the foundation laid out in front of you to a whole new level. ryva - you are amazing. black ice - thank you for inspiring me to write when i didn't think i had any more words left in me. liza - you've given me an opportunity that others only dream of, your star is going straight to the top. nicole - remember the atlas jams?! to everybody who ever went to wilhelmina's on thursday nights. to all the mc's graff writers, b-boys/girls, and dj's i've ever met, thank you.

cheryl & davina' - three black girls' productions, beginning 2002??!! tosin - you're the shit, and keep an eye on "that boy" for me. dewey, tonya marie, bernard collins, zenzelle, damon, stacey, steve, kevin covington, jam - you are the hippest supervisor imaginable, kia, damali, tarika, nakia - i wish it could be like it was, universal, alkia, lock - for the rose, ndgo, nasih, evonne - without your computer this book wouldn't exist, jackie, strangers on the street who i've solicited opinions from, lamar redcross. everyone who interviewed me and didn't hire me, pushing me to pursue my dreams. the whole philadelphia hip-hop community. all philly poets who write because they have to, not just to make a buck, or get a quick f@#k after the reading. anyone who feels they should be listed but aren't, y'all know i got a bad memory.

TABLE OF CONTENTS

INTRO	1
LYRICALLY GIFTED	2
FIRST CIPHER	4
STEREOPHONIC	5
IF I COULD RHYME	6
SOMETIMES I GOT ISSUES	7
MY LIFE	9
SHORTY	10
FOR MY SISTERS WHO'VE LOST THEIR VOICE	12
IS MATERIALISM ALWAYS BAD	13
THAT BOY	14
POEM FOR LEAH	16
JOURNAL ENTRY	17
LYRICALLY ILL?	18
FOR MY BIG BROTHER	19
PART OF ME	21
SPINNIN (FOR THE AVE)	23
INSPIRED	24
SHORTY 2	26
FOR HIP-HOP ACADEMIA	27
JUST STOP	30
BREAKIN (FOR THE AVE)	32
BAGGY BLUE JEANS	33
SHORTY 3	34
I DON'T WRITE AS MUCH	35

CONTENT CONTINUED

OPEN MIC?	36
DIGITAL COMMANDO	37
ELIXIR	38
YEAR IN REVIEW	39
THAT CULTURE	40
I HEARD HIP-HOP	42
WHY	44
UPDATED LOVE	46
MY PEEPS	48
SHORTY 4	51
FROM ONE TO ONE	52
BLACK MAN, BLACK MAN	53
CHESS MASTER	54
BUT FOR REAL THOUGH	55
FORTHCOMING	56
IF I COULD RHYME PART 2	58
MISSED THE 3	60
QUICK THAW	62
SPOKEN WORD SHORTY	63
LYRICALLY GIFTED (THE ORIGINAL)	64
THERE'S ALWAYS ONE	66
EXPLOSIONS	67
CNN ON HIP-HOP	68
DEFINITIONS	71

PISCES (FEB.19-MARCH 20): You won't serve time in hell for the bombs you drop this week, but, neither will you rack up Brownie points in the Book of Judgement. So, I guess your best motivation for doing what you're going to do will be for the sheer fun of it, for the righteous mischief, for the entertainment value of seeing everyone you encounter get up into the air by the tremors you send coursing through the earth beneath your feet.

INTRO

If hip-hop is going to maintain its power as a pure freedom of expression for our youth, we can ill afford to hide discussions behind ivy walls or inside books that our children wouldn't read, given a choice between picking up a book and running ball. What we need to succeed, if we are going to "keep this real" as a reflection of our lives, dreams and aspirations, is to reach the unreachable. Meaning those that have been unreachable to us.
Jay-Z gets them.
DMX gets them.
The streets get them.
Drugs get them.
Cops get them.
But as for us educated folks in denial about our bougie tendencies, trying to reach back and help, how do we help those who don't see a problem? An even bigger question is why should they come to us who occupy coffeehouses and art galleries. If your mom was getting high and your baby brother ain't had diapers in days, would you go to a coffeehouse or art gallery. Or would you go to your room, slamming the door and start blaring DMX and WHERE MY DAWGS AT!!!!!, thinking about ways that you can get out that house and have some fun. Chances are limited and we're running out of time, but our mission is not one in which we are allowed the luxury of failure.

Enjoy, better yet, discuss.
Naila Mattison-Jones

lyrically gifted

some of the most lyrically gifted
are quickly sifted
out of this whole music game
because their goals in life aren't to acquire fame
to them it's not about clout
chicks suckin dicks
and chemical lifts
being pimped by the industry
for a style that'll make a quick buck for a while
being fucked from behind cuz you can rhyme
maybe
cuz sometimes niggas get signed for the hell of it
make a quick sell of it and forget who they are
cuz somehow now they're stars
with no skills required
they have acquired their highest ideals
and those deals have taken meals
away from those that can truly bless the mic
and true sights been lost
because the urban youth that created this thing
are no longer the boss
cuz those with the right color skin can walk into a bank
or ask their fathers
for money to start a club or label
that'll have brothers fighting like cain and able
over a contract that wasn't wrote in ebonics
so now they broke
strugglin to get by
but why

when even those that trot along a path of original thought
can sometimes get caught
in the stagnation of verbal masturbation
braggin about how fly they are
when the content of their rhymes ain't always reachin that far
i cram to understand
how niggas can complain about the man
grandstandin from a house on the hill
givin the ghettoes nil
but that's not the real shit
cuz those with true hits
are heard on street corners or mix tapes
where real heads debate
who's got the baddest track
and there's no room to be wack
cuz if your skills ain't like that
you're quickly kicked to the curb
or thrown into the vault
with real mc's
whose only fault
was that they took the time to develop rhyme as an art
not settling on the worst part
or in it for material game
cuz when hip hop started
it ain't have shit to do
with commercial fame

First Cipher

2.08.95

i stand alone in a crowd of pure artists
and wonder whether or not i fit
then realize it doesn't matter
cuz if i "fit in"
i wouldn't be here in the first place
and where is "here"
here is amidst the music
the creativity
and the love
the rhythm
that flows through our souls
and escapes through those that are talented enough to release
it's all about the rhythm
it always has been
it always will be
flowin to the music
flowin to the beat
flowin to the spirit of the cipher til dawn

stereophonic

11.1.94

stereo sound
stereophonic surround sound -
    that's what that shit's called right?
comin at you from all angles
or is that you as you penetrate my mind entering all corners
sending me spinning around and around
looking for what's real
in particular, the real you
if that exists anywhere other than my mind
other than my heart
or are you just an image
virtual reality
complete with surround sound -
    that is what they call that shit, right?

if i could rhyme

6.24.99

if i could rhyme over bass lines
and keep time
with the speed in my mind
at which my thoughts travel
i would flow at 1,037 1/3 miles per hour
and people say i talk fast now
when i'm only going 500
in a 300 word per minute zone
i move quickly
so i can't be cloned
deliver it swiftly
to send your mind back home
to thoughts on a level
attuned to the highest science
minus
the spookisms
once again
it's me with the universal truisms

sometimes i got issues

7.11.98

there are times
when i have issues with hip-hop
because i got issues with mc's
who need to go back to school
and figure out just what they are masters of
when we're caught in the midst of economic enslavement
and brothers and sisters still can't congregate
in groups of more than five without police harassment

brothers and sisters are having children
before they know how not to be children themselves
but all these fools think there is to talk about
are their bitches
and their dicks
don't mutha fuckas get tired of that shit
wouldn't it hurt
to have a vision that myopic
is it that hard
to change the topic

can we free our minds and our behinds through our music
as opposed to lettin blood suckers use it
to keep crab niggas crabs
and we're all at the bottom of the barrel
just barely movin
and piled on top of one another in projects
don't you think it's time to stop the nonsense

obviously the experiment worked
inferior housing
inferior schooling
and deteriorating self images
equals a civil rights movement
moved backwards
and now rhymes reflect the times gone awry
so why try to elevate
why even contemplate freedom
only because
i don't know any other way
and you always want what you can't have

12.22.94

this is my life
it's all about the music
the rhythms and the rhymes
the lyrics
all those words and what they're saying
or what they say to me
how they swim inside my brain
flowing through my pen
and release themselves on paper
and then on those special occasions
when the shit is dope enough to express in a verbal form
and my mind goes into a frenzy
and the voice that keeps me sane
calls for that one last cry of freedom
from the pain of existence
and life as it exists for me on a level of consciousness
not touched by those that choose to sleep on the knowledge
that brought them into being
the knowledge that keeps me awake and aware
of all that surrounds me
especially the rhymes
especially the music
especially the music of life

records spin
to help release the everyday sin
of dreams deferred
by 9 to 5 work

FOR MY SISTERS WHO'VE LOST THEIR VOICE
1.11.98

Mother Fuckers still think
that women are inherently weak and wicked
so nigga i ask you
was she weak the other night
as you allowed your most vulnerable part
to penetrate her temple
causing you to moan and groan
begging for never ending bliss
was it wicked of a sister to carry the culmination of two
spirits for nine months
endure agonizing labor
for you to proclaim upon delivery
that, you have a son!
she must have been weak
not to slap your ass
like you contributed anything to that child
besides a chromosome
injected in approximately 2 minutes
maybe it was also wicked
of a black woman to stand by you
when you couldn't find a job
momentarily paying bills
cooking dinner
and never making you feel like any less of a man
it's definitely weakness
that would have a queen
listening to this type of shit
as opposed to being with a real sun
that isn't threatened
by his own reflection

is materialism always bad?
6.14.96

i want sapphire movado watches
and silk and lace swatches
forming canopies over my bed
with thoughts of me in your head
straight ruling your third eye
but never fucking up your vision
cuz all your thirsts i be quenchin
even though
i'm the one doin the lickin

sugar hill ain't just a vision for me
cuz i manifest reality
and lay out my destiny
while others try to slay with gun and swords
my words drop jaws
and have a nigga wishin
we were fuckin in my mental kitchen
cuz the chefs specialties be the shit
so i take another hit
and pass that shit

that boy
8.14.98

quiet as kept
hip-hop to me
is that lover
with whom i shouldn't of slept
you know the one
who can get inside you at times
and make you feel so good
even though the content of the rhymes
ain't always reflectin what they should
tellin me in one line
he wants nothin but queens
but in the videos
he's likely to be seen
with scantily clad
women easily had
that he was just dissin
hip-hop for me
be that one
offering long nights of fun
pulsating rhythms
til i come
to my senses
listening to the contradictions
thinkin this shit is like religion
or is it just the music
i be choosin

to fit my mood at the time
wantin to keep it and make it pure
clean up its nasty ways
so that together we can spend our days
trying to protect him from the street vengeance
that keeps sending his most gifted
to shallow graves
i crave the respect
born out of him taking responsibility for his children
give 'em what they need
and quit teachin 'em greed
while taking away a realistic self image
to settle for the stereotypic

yeah
hip-hop be that boy
i wanted to be my toy
but he was already committed to the street
and couldn't see to treat
me any different than he'd been treated
but refusing to be defeated
i chose to hold on
not only for my life
but for his

poem for leah

10.08.97

generally
my world consists of true, school and love
cereal, whole grain honey bagels and hip hop
not in any particular order
i think a lot about where i'm going with my life
i guess that's why i like being in transit so much
gives me a feeling of going somewhere
really having a destination
you're like my other side
watching our pieces is wild
you say all the things i wouldn't
but want to
you're like me without fear
i don't have to wonder what that would be like
i can watch you

journal entry

3.9.97

He paged me one day while I was at work, we were planning our first trip up to New York together to finalize this management shit. He was telling me about how, now the fifth got beef with biggie cuz one of them had been in Now Why that morning and heard some new shit where he's dissin the crew. So when we're up there he's gotta watch his back and be strapped, since he's from East, NY. The whole time I was trippin cuz it was the day after the thing with tupac's mom aired on dateline and all I could think about was my mother saying that's exactly why she didn't want me working with them guys that can't pull their pants up.

the night the soultrain awards aired
i was at the movies seein rhyme and reason
evidently
whether i was home or not
notorious was gonna be in my face
then i go to dc to see my father
and after seeing donnie brasco
wake up
and the b-i-g's been killed
now what
am i supposed to not care
cuz my associated crew had beef with him anyway
not care
because he had sent 'nough peeps to hospitals
not care
cuz i didn't respect him as a lyricist
or feel confused
cuz all in all
it's still another brother lost
over dumb shit

lyrically ill

i come lyrically ill
till i've had my fill
of mc's as appetizers
ready for the main course
with no remorse
of the mental slaying
cuz too many spend too much time playing
with they balls
and screamin - throw 'em up y'all

instead of fondling they testicles
they need to be sharpenin they manifestin skills
cuz ejaculation without procreation
is just sperm taking a meaningless vacation
and i'm wondering
when you first began to feel your castration
that has caused you to feel the need
to cum all over my brain lyrically
but it's possible that i too come
too cynically to my conclusions
about these obtrusions
attempting to penetrate my dome
but you can't touch
my present spiritual home

for my big brother
6.29.99

the privilege of being a little sister
is that i get to watch the flow
of women come and go
listening to the antics
of player haters
who resent the fact that
panties aren't thrown at them on the daily
but to you
the whole thing is just silly
chicks go into orgasm
as you walk in the room
and niggas get insecure
because they know they ain't quite that smooth
but you just take it all in stride
past roaming eyes
wondering in who's bed you lie
just so their gossiping can have some foundation
sitting there mentally gestating
on ways to bring you down
but being the hottest dj in town
you always rise above
filling atmospheres with love
and clucks without they heads on straight get shoved
to the background

when they can no longer relate
to late nights
and sporadic flights
across continents
for performances on demand
and new women
realizing you're the man
the privilege of being a little sister
is that
i get to watch the flow
of women come and go
and be close enough
to know who is staying

part of me
5.31.98

hip-hop makes up a large part
of who i am
it's the mentality
that makes me choose
life over destruction
and what would have me
prefer to be poor
over a life of corruption

all things ain't cute
and occasionally
niggas choose to shoot
but at least it's for a purpose
cuz sometimes
black rage comes to the surface
plights of poverty manifest
in trifling forms
reflected by the ways our queens dress
i stress
elevation for the masses
in the only culture that don't really care
about economic classes
as long as
you're true to self
no need to overcompensate

cuz you've got more than i do
cuz when the beat drops
we can all relate
cuz your crew reflects a lot about you
and where you're at
and life ain't about gats
and hoes
niggaz frontin
cuz they really moes

hip-hop is about art
and a creative way
to express the best part

spinnin (for the ove.)

fluidly freakin beats
vinyliciously
feeling the electricity
of tight bass lines
and pulsating minds
in tuned to the groove
knowing it's time to move
getting wet with anticipation
of turn table stimulation
the technics of this relaxation
require proper eye hand coordination
in preparation
for this year's
milk crate olympics

8.24.99

never a rhyme deferred
in my mind
it's just words occurred
forming patterns
that make weak mentals
turn to dark matter
don't like to splatter
on microphones
but not afraid to tell wack ones
to
go the hell home
don't touch it
if your full of bullshit
lacking creativity
or only dealing with
material reality
because the time now
is to transcend
with magnificent changes around the bend
but your thoughts are only linear
so give me your ear and i'll
teach you a lesson
outside of degrees
as it pleases me
i'll bring you off of your knees

as only i can
and show you the truth
of why god is the black man
so give me your hand
as i wrap fingers
one - two - three
around the mic so easily
and if you want to be a true mc
be aware of its great responsibility

shorty 2

what is this thing we call hip-hop
is it a way of life
or something found in a hair lock
can we understand the cultural relevance
of people standing on a corner
creating music mentally based
on a line
traveling like mind to like mind
telling stories of past, present and future times

for hip hop acedemia

Is hip-hop the writing on the wall
Of today's cultural renaissance
Is it the way the hand is sprawled
To balance a being
Engaged in a capoeira styled ballet
Is it a round piece of vinyl
Above a circular piece of metal
With felt sandwiched in between
Next to a sound transducer
Or
Is hip-hop dropping the science
Of what's on the minds
Of today's youth
Or a culmination of all the above
Combined with an African ancestry
That dictates the drum as a necessity

or...

could hip-hop be
niggas pissin on walls with spray cans
trying to make a name for themselves
feelin like a b-boy
caught in a whirlwind of break beats
in the midst
of a fly ass mix

while lyrics spill
the discourse of a way of life
that's the only freedom of expression some got
because being free to express yourself as an original in america
can cost you millions
in royalties, loyalties and lawyers fees
if you're not careful
in a landscape
where minds seek escapades
into bass lines
and high times
cuz city life
leaves a lot of livin to be desired
so retiring
from false attempts
to fit
into the system
i made the system build itself around me
cuz mainstream society
watches my clothes and my walk
for fashion trends
just like they stalk me
for the color of my skin
but hip-hop academia and afrocentrists can't understand me
cuz they keep looking without
for something that's within
because acknowledging it as part of your soul
means you should feel like shit
because you no longer control
its whereabouts
like a lost child
with a blind mother

just stop

10.21.98

stop drop and roll
ain't gonna save your soul
from eternal damnation
but not the kind that supposedly lead to christ's emancipation
not dealin with sin
but the state of mind you're in
falling into savage dens
of mindless melodies
and make believe felonies
no longer at ease
taking away our children's innocence
so they can no longer play in the breeze
cuz their minds are on freeze
from mental stagnation
because all your talk about bitches
is just lyrical masturbation
in overcompensation
for what you feel you lack
setting even lower standards on what it means to be black
and would you even be taken aback
if someone were to grab your ass
and insert
mr. sodomy king
there's no justification
for treating people as things for you to prey upon
not that you will be for long
careers like yours won't last forever

because some of us are wakening fast
better late than never
and taking over the airwaves
finally controlling what the media portrays as us
and fast acting like roach spray
we're turning common niggas to dust
so trust
your ass is next
because it's time to remove the likes
of a d - m ...

breakin (for the ave.)

b-boys and girls
do flips and twirls
patterned after dances
from lands
they've only glanced at
on maps

they bend backs
and drop knapsacks
to place they claim on hip-hop
usin cardboard boxes
as escape
from schools of hard-knockses

baggy blue jeans
2.10.95

i saw this b-boy the other day
boldly boppin down the street
in baggy blue jeans
big black boots
and a baseball cap pulled down
so as to hide
his bright, beautiful, brown eyes
he was a sight to behold
with his badass attitude
escaping from every pour in his body with every stride he took
and i wanted him to be my bold, black man
and let me show him how to love in that sweet
sensuous, sexually satisfying way that only a black woman can
but keep boppin b-boy
because though those large luscious lips
cause my mind to drift drowsily into that dream world
where fantasy and fulfillment become one
i have no time for b-boys with big dreams
and no plans
only revolutionaries
trying to take a stand

shorty 3

the frugal mc
can't break bread
unless it's with equality
dub a borrowed cd from a friend
but'll buy wax with a vengeance
if the need is urgent
lyrically divergent
chillin on a spurred moment

i don't write as much

1.01

how can i devote my attention
to the bullshit of hip hop
when i need to notice my son's first two teeth
or maybe
how can i not
because he's gonna get to that age
where he's listening to the radio on his own
...who knows what it'll be by then
maybe ended
transformed
or blended
into an even greater pile of garbage
than it already is
...as if that's possible...
but if it is
the results could be deadly
minds need to be cultivated not tenderized
and we consistently close our eyes
to the evils that niggas do
so we can gain false pride
by seeing another brown face
in a place
of prominence
my
oh
my
oh
my
i don't write as much
cuz obviously
if i'm to raise a sentient being in this society
i've got a lot of work to do

open mic?

6.9.99

i watched the dkny host
heard the bullshit dropping out of people's mouths
that i was being forced to listen to
and thought
this venue is not for you
maybe it's me
used to hip-hop niggas
with baggy clothes
mc dreams
and ghetto realities
lookin for places to feel themselves
or crowded rooms
where people congregate at the back to swap stories
and greet those they haven't seen since the last reading
while musiq blesses the microphone in ways that make me jealous
or black ice, skates into a rhyme
freezing a moment in time

my mind travels
happily chasing words into whatever forests
in which they'll lead
towards butterflies, mushrooms or grass, without the papers
i feel free
because i trust conduits to be careful
with their judgment
and not rape my ears
spewing semantics with no context
in which to impregnate

digital commando

mc's lack proper training to command microphones
because without knowledge of history
they tend to become oral clones
cuz nowadays
dj's get degrees by burning cd's
and mixing mp3's
not willing to dig through vinyl crates
they lay and wait in cyberspace
plugged into napster
musical skills take a step back
while you're
searching...
searching...
for what you heard was hip
hopped to it quick
jumped on it like a dick
proceeding to take a lick
but wackness prevailed
should've checked your email
or gone to live365.com
now you're forced to exist under a nom
de plume
until true talent is conceived
calling yourself an mc
when you're freestyle largely underachieves

elixir

2.21.98

hip-hop is an elixir
taken to ease the growing pains of life
i walk along a bass line
tight as me
in a pair of 7/8 jeans
it's a release
not like r&b
havin you all in tears
hip-hops that stuff that gets you high
reminiscin on smoke filled clubs
smoke filled lungs
and vibrations pulsating the whole buildin
nobody cared that there weren't any fire exits
or coat checks
we grumbled about being patted down
but knew
we'd rather be that
than shot
hip-hop's an elixir
to wash away the bad
and only leave the good of the universe
and when bullshit became intertwined
the hip-hop left
and commercial rap replaced it
until it was safe to come back
and it always will
that's how you know it's hip-hop

year in review
1.09.98

i manifested most of my dreams
wearin locks
a head wrap and some jeans
knowin most niggas just want what's in between
but they'll never see it
chasin the poor part of perfection
attemptin to satisfy weak erections
with no direction
and life to them is just a meaningless float
niggas be on the corner
with a constant gloat
unless they "hard"
then maybe a snarl
but what for
will that knock down the door of confusion
maybe a mentality transfusion
but who wants to be left with what you got
i think not
but warmer nights are comin
maybe this year we'll stop the gunnin
and runnin
away from our true nature
that only wants to be free

that culture
5.27.98

hip-hop be the culture
that thinks it bore itself
neglecting it's mothers
and calling its daughters dick suckers
never realizing
that women hold the purchasing power
buying up all this trash
that makes our self image sour
cuz it's in a sister's nature
to support a brother
even after he's raped her
on track
and his beat was all jacked
there's still love
cuz he claims to be attempting to accomplish something
though she struggles to understand it's significance
beyond mind pollution
mentally searching for solutions
to the problem of wholistic incompatibility
because hip-hop can't possibly
think it can be saved
in it's present state
about to die in a shallow grave
because he won't take his mother's milk
and receive the nourishment of life
not found in smoky clubs

where young white whores
frequently give themselves freely
because they're used to being subjugated
and black dicks make them feel elated
while a sister waits on the sidelines
for brothers to see
who they are
and what we be

i heard hip hop

7.10.98

i heard hip-hop at footwork
not in the swift lyrical skill
of a group known as ill
though they certainly blessed the mic
in a way that would advise all but the very best
to stay home and rest

i heard hip-hop
not necessarily from the poetic sounds
of some of philly's finest
whose clairvoyance cleared the stage
as it was blessed by lyrical sage

i heard hip-hop
in the drum and calabash
that was made to dance
and signal to home
that it was time to return
it called all to their center
it screamed
FREE MUMIA!!!!
FREE MUMIA!!!!
without a verbal word
and it was hip-hop
because it was life
and hip-hop is life
for people on the verge of death
the last cries of freedom
because we don't have to go down
we can

refuse and resist
we can drum talk with a calabash
we can drum talk with our heartbeats
we can drum talk with the drum
we can talk
without speaking a word
and it's hip-hop
because it's life
to a people who know the real and want to stop the deal
that's going down
and it's time to take a stand
and do more than just frown
upon those that talk the talk
but won't risk losing their mental security enough to fight
it's time to be
either part of the solution
or just become a cop
or any other outright genocidal factor of original people
so i know your ass ain't about nothing from the door

don't front like this is real to you
if in your heart it's not
because devils will always try
but they can't destroy the energy that brings life
or hip-hop

why?
1.10.97

why is it
that all niggas do
is go around quotin mothafuckas
from
scholarly
ne-groes
to
corner thugs
it's like
peeps ain't had an original thought
since 1983
so what
puffy and lil kim
gotta be that national spokesperson
for the destruction
of hip-hop?
i gotta say it
cuz some of y'all gotta listen to your lyrics
check your mics
and see what you're establishin
keepin it real
or manifestin positivity
it's an original mind state
understand that
thoughts travel at a powerful rate
as they are transferred
throughout
the earth's atmosphere
who do yours belong to?

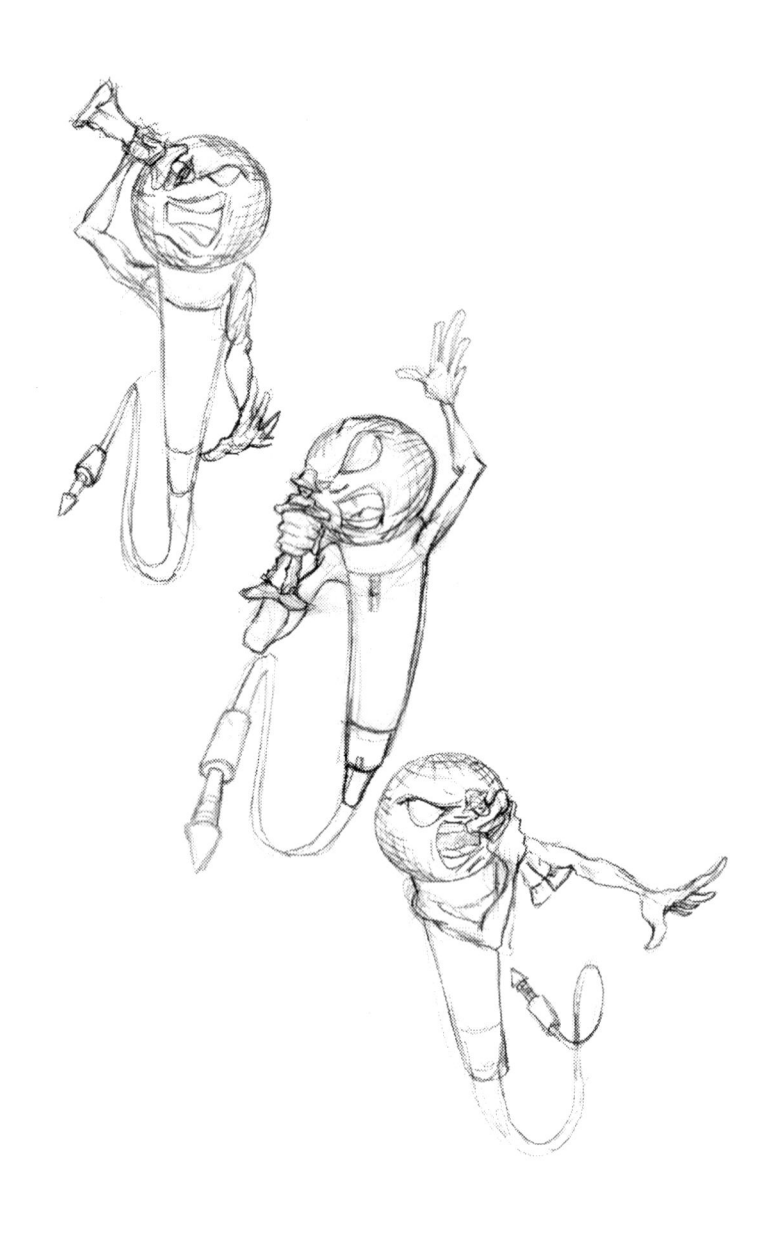

updated love

it was a long engagement
courtship was sweet
i knew it would last
from the way we danced in the streets

traveled to urban art galleries
and partook of vibrational stimulation
you spoke sweet words at times
but mostly just fun and explorations
of things to come

had me convinced of how fly you are
with your braggadocious style
never minding that every now and then
you'd call me a bitch or a hoe
because that wasn't the foundation of what we had
so i stayed and agreed
for better or for worse
not realizing the curse
that layed ahead
i was still wading in our marital bed
but break beats brought chaos
and it became all about you
and whatever extracurriculars you chose
to let take your focus
so it was all hocus pocus

no longer grounded in reality
but you keep lettin outsiders tell me
your keepin it real
while i'm supposed to sit by
and watch your slow death quicken
grief stricken
i try to reach out

and remind you what i once was
but your vision's clouded
by ghetto fab thugs
so i wait for the truth
of who you are to surface
remembering that for better or for worse
i agreed to stick with this

oh hip, oh hop
have you gone astray
oh where, oh where can you be
with your mind on thugs
and your soul on doe
will you ever return
back to me

my peeps (rewrite)

12.12.98

poets pervade my mind
painting pictures as vivid as marvel
from dc to germany
life unravels
like a ball of twine
all encompassed within the rhyme
words travel through the jellies of our culture
not selling a magic potion
to help ease Davina's notion
of worlds turning on themselves
and wars born out of internal hells
or heavens
cuz a sister as sharp as Tonya Evans
takes you to the curb
with a verb
or a noun
while Jill Scott'll get down
with a funk sound
on any verbal outing
and much opposed to those spouting
oratory bullshit
Stephanie Renee' comes again
with another hit
voice as smooth as butter
or as forewarning as your mother
because Zenzelle can be
that goddess black woman
or a sensual sheba offering spiritual seduction

but don't none of it matter
to miss ruby flow
as Yolanda plants mental flowers
beautiful words that bloom in the heart
of 15 years olds
off to the proper start
telling a room full of her elders
that until she found that last page
they had to wait
to help us understand
the weight of Rich Medina's world
because things fall apart
in ways that Chinua Achebe forsought
but most africans are too disconnected
to see the direct lineage that stretches
from the drum
to hip-hop
and we must continue to resist
while Bernard's super niggers still exist
helping to erase blacks from the list
of those who will see
the coming of the new age
while listening to Ayana
i feel the quiet rage
of incidents that my body will physically heal from
but my spirit may take a lifetime
to overcome
maybe if i smoked an el on a mountain top

i'll learn the lessons
of the blessins
given by Trapeta Mayson
just in the realm of conversation
forget about the verbal libation
cuz my imagination runs away
at the way Dewey comes from the dome
and some sisters longingly moan
when leaving his presence
but in all it's just the essence
of black poetics

the original mind
sees all
hears all
and speaks all
on an open mic
because every time a mouth is opened
we've given birth to new life

shorty 4

where was i
when hip-hop turned into diamonds, tattoos and bling blingin
i must have been lost
in mazes of lyrical mysticism
soakin up poetical witticism
and failed to notice the changing tide
before it washed over me
flooding our collective conscious
with corrupted, corny, categorically desuetude crap
being passed off as hot shit
what gets labeled as hits
is quite remised
they seem to have missed the point
beyond being paid and laid

from one to one

12.17.98

hey mr. dj
sexy mother fucker standing there
each hand caresses a turn table
and a long, slim cigarette
dangles precociously from your lips
i would prefer if it was an el
but the thought of a potential taste still arouses me
if i get to feel those finger tips
make me drip
mr. dj
got me turned inside out
and the feeling is
something like a flight in the sky
got me kind of hypnotized
but i'm not pursuing
until it's been said
waitin for you to make your move
continually feelin you
putting me in the groove

blackman, blackman

i like to hear ryva
call out to a black man
but there are times when
to the untrained eye
that appears to be an oxymoron
there's always
so many more important things
for brothers to be
than black men
they'd rather be
your nigga
or your dog
i guess that qualifies me
to be your bitch
word
i don't recall
seeking that title
i may have asked
if i could be your earth
make you my sun
and the traveling that i would do around you
might make you my god
but
you took advantage
and because of your own
lack of awareness
became my devil
but at the time
you didn't know
that the earth spits fire
when it needs to reach higher

Chess Master

3.15.96

it's a set up
a pawn moves out
innocently enough
on a reconnaissance
mission for the knight

watching your opponent's moves
from an angle where you are
in the game
as opposed to merely controlling it
changes one's perception

a bishop cattycorners
leaving a queen momentarily
open for attack
but always thinking ahead

one rook sets up defense
while another queen plots victory

the king sees walls
closing in on him
on all sides even too late
for suicide bombing mission

check mate.

rabbits and cows

it's very obvious that he
feels insecure about you
when he's around me
why is that?

so, do you even want
a real woman or are you
just enjoying screwing?

i'm bored with
my partners i always
want what i can't
obtain i need
the challenge

so, when are
we fucking?

but for real though

i am
not to be defined by simple minds
because my energy flows past these asses
and into mine own
space time continuum
where some will never see
anything but 1/16 of a glimpse of me
am i
still making sense
or have i lost myself in spiritual rhetoric
but i heard
that y'all spoken word mothafuckas like shit abstract
and maybe my realness
is what would cause my audience to get lost
because most times i extend
way past gettin and givin draws

FORTHCOMING

11.07.99

poor righteous
incarcerated sons
travels as vessels
keeping businesses fluid
while their minds turn numb
from
lack of influence
not able to exercise their rights as human beings
because dumb niggas allow themselves to get caught
in a justice system that only sees them as inanimate things
better than robots
because the parts to build them
were free
simple as shitty education
no parental upbringing
and radio heroes
telling them nothing is more important than money
funny
them niggas got some shit already - legally
which is not going to be affected
by whether or not
you go to jail
trying to acquire it
and eminem is every white boy's role model
cuz now

he can have sex with black women
while black men pursue white chicks
livin the american multicultural dream
i be wantin to scream
but
what good does that do
in a void
already filled with noise pollution
so my mind seeks solution
made the decision a long time ago
that my forthcoming seed
will be
nothing less than a queen
or king
a living model of righteousness
because this vessel carries life
for its people
because poor righteous suns
ain't got time to waist
on incarceration
or hanging with slow ones
screaming about reparations
i pour libations
seeking counsel
with my enlightened ancestors
on answers
to brighten dark times

if i could rhyme 2

12.07.99

a lot of niggas like to bullshit
in they lyrics
but with my mental
and my seed
we ain't tryin to hear it
cuz while
Nas is like...
And Na Na be like...
Naila is simply amazingly skilled
verbally assaulting assholes
most times it's a quick kill

i don't need to give you a catchy delivery
because if you listened carefully
you'd realize that the words i'm sayin be
pure liquid testaments
of truth
undiluted
so they can melt down
all the places where you've been polluted

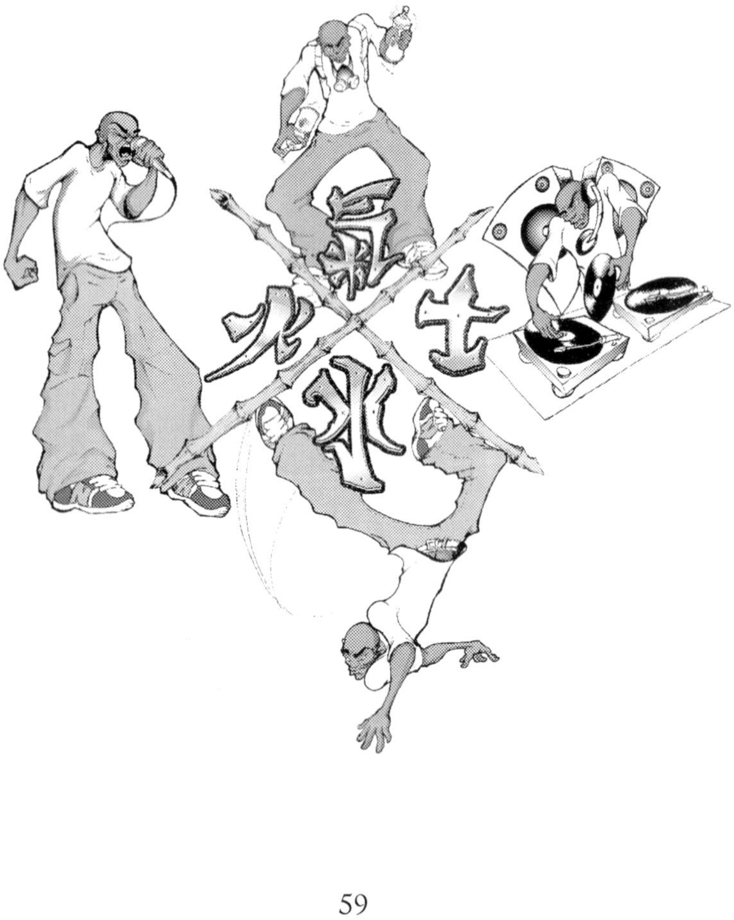
氣
火
土
水

i missed the 3
10.22.96

on the way to see you
from school
i decided to walk
(more because i missed the 3 than anything else)

while walking
i played a cultural tourist
contemplating hip-hop
as the ghetto
and the ghetto as hip-hop
and realized
that hip-hop can't be the ghetto
because the geographic boundaries
in which we choose to live
are more than just the youngsters
standing on corners
in lyrical ciphers
building their skills
and deciding
which life
they're going to live

it's more than the soul
of the elders congregating
on their porch steps
or sitting in the bars
that the youngsters know better
than to go in uninvited

more than the alto-sax
of the 40ish women
who still know how
to bounce their hips
respectfully
but enough to make a young boy
wanna learn

it's larger than the r&b of the girls
in their playground
mixing thoughts of double dutch
with the boy next door

so
as i think on all this
a car rides by
with street dreams
blaring out of the speakers
that really don't have as good a quality
as the driver thinks they do
and it causes me to reconsider
the ghetto as hip-hop
or
hip-hop as the ghetto

quick throw
12.30.98

beats warm my mind
while whole worlds
are carved out on wax
no words
just sounds painting melodies
sounds like scripture to me
an untrained ear
with an unbridled mind
i write in pictures
i hear music in pictures
and write now i'm picturing
you and me
grooving in the same time and space
it'd be nice
cuz lately
it just feels like
we haven't even been in the same galaxy
where you at
where am i going
and how come our spirits only come together and collide
as opposed to
creating an event horizon unto themselves
like they used to
where am i going
and can i take you on the ride?
or do i just need to do the me thing
and hope i catch you
On the next rotation

spoken word shorty

this whole notion of performance poetry
seems to have fallen into a black whole
where no one quite knows
what's going to be at the bottom
when all things truly become one
but until we get to that point
there's a long spiral downward
dope ass writers
get downplayed
for fake ass performers
that'll bite a style in a minute
to get applause from people
that ain't think shit about poetry
before 1997
and eleven
more talented peeps
get lost in the trenches each night
waiting for their turn on the mic

lyrically gifted (original)

6.28.98

some of the best mc's i know
ain't even trying to get paid
because having skills to them
is more than a show of who they can lay
and play
head games with
arbitrary bitches
just suckin their dicks ain't
what they're about
and record labels trying to front on cash
and their peoples turning into
big backstabbin asses

even those that trot along a path of original thought
can sometimes get caught
in the stagnation
of lyrical masturbation
braggin about how fly they are
but their lyrics ain't always
reachin that star
and scars are left on their psyche
because they might be
just that much more sophisticated
if their minds hadn't debated
the exact calculation of payment received
for lyrics achieved
born out of natural talent

now hoed to the highest bidder
but consider
the less pressured artist of the brush
no need to rush
painting pictures on canvas
but only the mc is blessed enough
to paint picture with the word
heard
on street corners
or mix tapes
that real heads debate
over who's the flyest
in the midst of hip-hop crisis
cuz some of the best mc's i know
don't want to deal with
the problems of the dough
the shadiness of the industry
for them
ain't the place to be
because at their present place
they can dwell freely
choose to bless an open mic
or not
if niggas sound trite

but it's sad
because the peeps i know
that got the best lyrics
keep it so dl
the masses will never hear it

there's always one

10.06.95

beats boom
out of large black boxes
and the frequencies fuck with my mind
while i'm
fucking you
two worlds collide
but nothing less than orgasms
signify
the collisions
love invades lust
and i try to catch my breath
but i feel your tongue
touch the tip
of my left nipple
oceans flow through my body
as your divine eye
is no longer inside me
it is me
because i wouldn't know
how to let go
even if i wanted
lust invades love
as my physical presses itself against yours
proving that
the sun and moon
at times
are so close
they're one

explosions
12.13.95

while i put pen to paper
you put bullet to chamber
and expect something good to flow
through the barrel of my gun i explode
in bursts of
    blue
            black
even purple if the mood occurs
and you explode through a shot in the dark
and anticipate my arrival
wanting my body
but needing my mind
and as i make love to you
trying to calm your restlessness
my own spirit is left unfulfilled by your greed
as you drain my emotions through your tunnel of darkness
into the abyss i go
fighting the whole way
but
still
going
down

cnn on hip hop
6.12.01

okay
little mr. whiteboy
cnn reporter

obviously your research department
has internet access
but your perspective
denies you the only thing
your skin color can't grant you
your divide and conquer tactics
will not work on the creators
of rap hits
because they were already used to it
so let's set it straight
hip-hop is a diverse culture
rap is a diverse language used
within the culture
and I respect it's dirty south dialects
with skill
as much as I respect those comin
from North Phil
and I guess your problem would come
from being born into a culture
that only understands dichotomy
and chaos
not harmony
and balance

Allow us
to not care if a bunch of white kids are now
into hip-hop
so the lyrics have to be legislated against
the same way
it took a white boy to die from crack
before they really decided selling drugs
should be federal offense
we're tired
of trying to justify our existence
to people
that only want to be able to control it
without understanding
just consistently reprimanding
like we can't take care of ourselves
so no wI'm pretty much fed up
and
jake taffer you can GO TO HELL!!!!

definitions

1. **mc**-abbreviation for Emcee; one who has the ability to write well thought out, diverse ryhmes in addition to being able to   hold their own in a freestyle session. short for master of ceremonies, microphone commander, etc..If you can't freestyle you can still be a good lyricist, as long as you're writing your own stuff, but you can not be a MC if you can't hold your own , on the spot, with no rehearsals.

2. **vinyliciously**-okay, I really just made this one up, but the context should explain itself.

3. **nom de plume**-french for pen name or alias

These are my own personal definitions , but feel free to air all grievances at lyricallygifted.com

naila who?

A true lover and supporter of Hip Hop culture, Naila's Hip Hop inspired poetry has been used as an educational tool to discuss cultural politics at community centers, correctional facilities and high school classrooms. She is the Associate Producer of The Avenue, a Billboard Award winning show and has worked with a number of local TV stations in Philadelphia including DUTV, WTVE and The Box. Naila teaches video production classes to middle and high school students, and is a freelance videographer. She resides in Philadelphia with the two men in her life, her husband and son.

For More Info. or to *Order Books*
Check these Sites

www.lyricallygifted.com
www.impactpublishing.net
www.fyos.com/nmattison-jones.htm
www.creators-child.com/manifest/reckasto.html
www.amazon.com